The Long Way Home

A Collection of Travel and Nature Poetry

Abigail Cheek

Dedication

This collection of poetry is dedicated to to all who find beauty in unsuspecting places, to the travelers, and to the wildflowers they pick up along the way.

Preface

As we travel through life, the beauty and awe of the natural and unnatural world can sometimes find us in the most unlikely of places. This collection of poetry was inspired by places and bits of nature that strike the mind in a menagerie of ways and ply imagination in its most quiet moments. I hope these small dalliances of my mind can take you the long way home and maybe back around again. May we all find the beauty in our beholding eyes, and every now and then dip into unknown territory before we land back to the familiar.

Acknowledgements

Deepest thank you to those who consistently make the journey of life ever more interesting, even if I cannot mention them all in just a few lines: Garrett, Lily, Pamela, Beth, Tina, and Ingra. Without each of you some journeys might have ended long before they began. Another special thank you to influential teachers and mentors over the years: Kim, Connie, Ann, Dr. Josey, Dr. Beasley, and Brad. Your lifelong belief in students and dedication never go unnoticed. Finally, love to all the travelers, witnesses of nature, and the God that created them.

1. Shades of Green

The trees have an iridescent green glow to them
This time of year.
Small mountain roads are growing wild flowers
With crippling creeks and steady rivers.
If I reach out at just the right moment it feels
As if I might become part of the rocks
That the fresh waters are tumbling over.
Maybe if I dip deep enough in the spring water
It could wash my old wounds.
There valleys are below full of grasses
Already standing two feet high.
Just enough to tickle your legs
Once summertime.
The monarchs are fluttering just above
Honeysuckle vines off the ledges.
Even the hawk and raven dance among the shade
Of the pine and oak limbs.
I breathe in, then out, but could it be
That those mountains are breathing back?

2. Watching Water

Watching the water becomes easier
When you realize
Whether you are there by its side or not
Water will ebb and flow
With its rocky bed beneath.

Watching the water becomes gentler
When the way you breathe matches
Whether ripples stray farther in and out
Water will ebb and flow
With your spirit there or not.

3. Take the Long Way

Keep your head down honey,
Don't tell them you're running,
Or that you still have miles to go.

Never tell your secrets,
Or how you mean it,
When you say you'd rather be alone.

Take the long way home,
Drive until you're so far gone,
That it seems a world away,
And you can't remember why you stayed.

They won't know how to take you,
They'll know how to break you,
Those words are going to cut like ice,

Only one will listen,
And he's back home wishing,
That he knew where you were right now.

Take the long way home,
Drive until you're so far gone,
That it seems a world away,
And you can't remember why you stayed.

I want to learn,
I want to fly,
But most of all I want to drive.

Take the long way home,
Drive until you're so far gone,
That it seems a world away,
And you can't remember why you stayed.

4. Tops

We spy mountain tops,
Gently run our hands over the vast
Flora and Fauna
Sticking up from the faces on skimming tops,
It almost feels as if there are beds of green and blue,
In the distance sharing their secrets and waiting,
For a passerby to ask to touch them.

5. The Lighthouse

The most naturally beautiful place
I have visited as of yet,
Is the Honduras.

We were on one of those cruises,
The ones that privileged people take
Just so they can see and taste a little bit of
Outside the U.S.

The town just beyond the port we stopped at?
Devastating.
I had not witnessed that kind of poor before.
It was as if we stepped into some other world,
One burdened by some cataclysmic event I knew nothing
of.
I wept all the way up the mountain,
In some taxi I thought I might die in.

The scenery surrounding the town itself?
Ethereal.

Trees are in a shade of green and flowers in colors
I had never seen before and never since.
Water was a hue I'm sure heaven even
Demands of its waters.

What irony that such a place
Could have to of the most direct contrasts.
What irony that I would weep for the children in the
street,
Then lie on a private beach wondering how I got there.

On the way out of the port,
Back to the boat,
We stopped at some street sellers by the docks.
Every place I visit I like to find little pieces of art.
Not the kind that had been reprinted and sold for
thousands,
No, the kind from artists who live by their craft little by
little.

A man was selling small paintings of many different
varieties
At a small cart.
He couldn't speak English, but a woman sitting with him
could.
I offered him some American money,
More than what each small painting had labeled on

them,
Not enough to damage my funds at all.

He turned to speak to the woman,
She said I should take two.
"No, No," I said, "That is for his labor."
She and he thanked and told some short story,
About how he uses the money to provide for his family.

Maybe that was true.
Maybe he had several children to care for at home,
And a constant dwindling pot of money.
Maybe they lied.
Maybe he used his money for a smoking habit
Or to drink copious amounts of alcohol each night.
Didn't matter. The art was beautiful anyway.

The painting was small and contained mostly dark hues,
Navy, Royal Blues, Yellows.
Nothing like what I had seen that day.
It was simply a lighthouse at nighttime.

6. Favored

I waited for a hero
The help never came.
No distress signal here,
Statues will stand in the rain.

Pain is like a beacon,
Call the higher self home.
Keep the bitter taste away,
Continue on to roam.

Me and God like the birds better,
They sing throughout the mourning.
Despite the loss of summer,
Their wings will keep them flying.

7. Waltzing

I saw too much malice,
At too young an age.
Now I have demons that follow,
A shiny black entourage.

They are not like yours,
No, not sad clowns that miss the punchline,
That cannot get the act right until the crowd is gone,
And left with nothing but their sorrows.

These clever silver belles and golden gents
Remind me of Lucifer and Lilith.
Once the most beautiful and musical of them all,
Then their claws became too strong.

Oh no,
My demons waltz.
They waltz in gorgeous attire like leaves falling in
autumn.
Floating like ghostly figments but all too real.

Sometimes I like to stop and gaze at them,
Yet I dare not for too long.
Then I'll be waltzing too.

8. La Luna

"Mommy why is the moon following us?"
Perhaps she needs a friend,
And can only find them in the solitude
Of her favorite time.

"Mommy why is the moon following us?"
Perhaps her lover the sun,
Left her alone in the sky for a while,
But knowing he may not return she couldn't stand the
star signs.

"Mommy why is the moon following us?"
Because perhaps in the silence of space,
The only thing keeping her alive,
Is us.

9. Magna

The wind unfurled it's wings,
The trees begin to sway,
Suddenly I hear music.

There are sorts of beasts that make noise
In the night and in the day.
They fly on feathered bones.

A favorite of these;
Strong red-tailed hawks,
Watch over my family and I.

Once In a trance I met one,
She even gave me her name,
Magna.

10. Chaos

The mind is much like the chaos that exists in nature,
Whether we realize it or not; we appreciate the chaos,
Sometimes from inside our safe homes,
Sometimes through a thin tent in the wilderness.
But with the enamored love of chaos still comes the rain.
And thunder, and lightening, and smoke, and fire.
What chaos brings is the unknowing,
And the unknowing is not always a friend.
I can stand and watch the world and its wonders fall
apart,
Then slowly stitch itself back together.
Sometimes it does,
Sometimes it doesn't.
The mind is much the same.

11. Secret Gardens

Since I child I have obsessed,
Especially under times of great duress,
My little bookish dreams of old,
Are what my mind does solid hold.

I read it in a book somewhere,
That you could sometimes disappear,
Within the solid garden walls,
And never once again be called.

These secret gardens had iron keys,
To which I could hide anywhere I please,
Under a stone, or behind a brick,
Seems like a clever childlike trick.

I always thought if I had a say,
To where my secret garden lay,
It might be a place peaceful and calm,
A place where all nature could roam.

With endless lilies standing by,
A sweet wooden swing to help me fly,
Stoney paths with no real end,
All the manner of flowers tend.

Tiny animals would silently trail,
Behind my whisper of footsteps frail.
We would dance together soon,
Underneath the pale blue moons.

There would always be quiet music at play,
Though from what instrument I could not say,
Only me waltzing with some apparition,
To some musical of haunting rendition.

12. What winter Feels Like

Hell is cold.
I think every Bible in the world might be lying about hell
being hot.
Call me blasphemous.
My skin burns with annoyance at the thought,
Of any one tiny snowflake touching my skin.

No matter that each snowflake is unique,
Like a beautiful human finger print.
That may be God's work,
But the devil is in the cold.

May be that it is pretty to look upon,
There is a beautiful quiet to it as it absorbs most sound.
Ah but, there is also a pretty and quiet road,
Paved with good intentions, and goes straight to hell.

13. Even if

How does your garden grow?
Does it creep through side walks put on top of it?
Does it persist even if the water doesn't fall from the
sky?
Resilient things are more enchanting than anything else.

Even though the rose has thorns,
It can produce one of our favorite flowers.
Even if you have to trim it back each year,
It comes back better the next season.

They call them weeds sometimes,
The dandelions, the purple nettles,
Coming up through sidewalk cracks.
Weed is the wrong word for such a wishful strength.

I hope the same for you,
I hope that even if they bury you too deep,
Even if they lay concrete over your resting place,

I hope you push up the brightest daisies.

19

14. Language of Trees

There are those that say they've found,
That plants make their own special sound.
Far below and higher than we humans hear,
They share their songs and stories near.

Through vibrations in the ground,
And in the air all around,
The plants speak secrets to each friend,
So they can keep their deep roots end.

Listen closely,
Closer now.
Can you tell?
Can you hear their nature's spell?

I hear them sometimes on the wind,
Just when I need a thought to spin.
They swear fealty to only me,
Because I know the language of trees.

15. Power Grid City (NYC)

One of the most lively places I've seen,
Looks like its own power grid from the sky.
Most lights stay on for eons,
Some twinkle just for those who love them.
NYC is alive.
The whole city itself breathes light and fire and industrial
tunes.
Almost like a constant circus act, the tightrope one,
You cannot possibly look away.
Cars, trains, and planes play their noise all night,
It doesn't matter, not in a high rise.
Down on these streets,
Each one has a different life of its own.
My favorites are the ones with theaters on them.
Where play actors, singers, and dancers twirl,
Different stories come to life and end too quickly.
Time is crucially irrelevant here,
Why go to bed when the lights are pulling you towards
city center at midnight?

16. Staying Still

What a tragedy it would be,
To never move or never see?
All the wonders passed the lines,
That you've drawn inside your mind.

What benefit would you keep,
If you never gazed upon the sea?
With all it's massive strength and wave,
All the memories you could save.

What more work could you get done,
If through forests you never run?
See the leaves changing in the fall,
Never hearing the hoot owl's call.

You're fear will keep you staying still,
No wandering in power of will,
What a tragedy it would be,
To never move or never see.

17. Dry Heat

The heat here is dry,
As in the kind that doesn't burn,
But simply washes over the skin in the wind,
To keep you aware of where you are.

Back home the heat is pouring water,
Water from the air,
Water from the lakes and ponds,
Water from even the trees.

But the heat here is dry.
Something tells me I could survive a little easier,
If I stayed here in the summer rather than back home,
Though I might miss the water a bit.

They say there are cowboys here,
But in the big cities I see none,
Not really,
They have nice hats but I think they do not know how to
wrangle anything.

The wide open spaces are nice on a drive,
The cities hold much more light and fun.
History in these places are old and fascinating,
For one that wishes to time travel.

18. Autumn Ground

We have come into this house,
That is not our own.
But the floor is paved,
With liquid gold.

When red flakes fall,
From a windy sky,
And birds then whistle,
Autumn is nigh.

The gourds crawl slowly,
Upon the ground,
I hear the whisper,
Of a chill breeze sound.

There's sunset colors,
Falling off the trees,
All of us can feel,
The gentle peace.

19. Tik Tok, Tik Tok

Tik tok, Tik tok,
The steady beat of the old wood clock.
I used to hate the ugly whine,
Of a measure of the time.

We are getting older now,
And the steady beat that I have found,
May not be so bad after all,
If I control what the mind enthrall.

I think now the chime,
Of the measure beat of time,
Rocks me quicker off to sleep,
Before my thoughts can steep too deep.

Funny how things do change,
Stranger still how they remain the same.
Tik tok, tik tok,
The steady beat of the old wood clock.

20. Nighttime Blues

We could walk close to the edge of the world together.
Where the daytime fades into night and the stars come
out to play.
You could tell me you've never been this close to
eternity.
I could tell you that we were still too far away.

Old times used the stars to tell the future and the past,
I use them to make selfish wishes on the off chance one
is listening.
I've seen many stars fall, sideways across the nighttime
blues.
Maybe that is when God can hear my tiny soul
whispering.

21. All The Places We Have Not Been

All things end and begin again,
The journey home calls on a friend,
Places far can stand to wait,
We should not tempt the hand of fate.
Have a rest while watching a passerby,
Not bothered as to when and why.
Been running off somewhere to hide.

www.ingramcontent.com/pod-product-compliance
Lightning Source LLC
Chambersburg PA
CBHW061321140726

47998CB00006B/2498